Rational

THOUGHTS

Common Sense Improvements to Life in America

SAM GALANIS

PAGE PUBLISHING
Conneaut Lake, PA

First originally published by Page Publishing 2024

ISBN 979-8-89157-805-0 (pbk)
ISBN 979-8-89157-836-4 (digital)

Printed in the United States of America

CONTENTS

ON FDIC INSURANCE

In October 2008, the Federal Deposit Insurance Corporation increased the level of insurance from $100,000 to $250,000. You would need over $350,000 today to buy what $250,000 bought in 2008. Or put another way, $250,000 in 2008 dollars is worth $180,000 today.

The bottom line: the FDIC insurance should be inflation-adjusted.

BANK SAVINGS ACCOUNTS

Available research has shown that countries with higher rates of savings have been able to grow their economies faster than countries with lower rates.[1]

So you pay taxes on income earned, then deposit some of that money into a bank savings account, and you pay taxes again on the interest earned. It would help both you and the economy and encourage saving if Uncle Sam is not your continuing partner in your bank savings account.

The bottom line: make interest earned on bank savings accounts not taxable up to the FDIC deposit insurance limit.[2]

---

[1] MoneyLion by Jeannine Macini, "Why Savings Are Important: For Your Finances and the Economy," March 23, 2023.

[2] Currently $250,000.

A STABLE DOLLAR

In 1960, your hamburger cost 21¢ at a diner and 15¢ at McDonald's. When McDonald's introduced the "Big Mac" in 1967, it cost 45¢. Today a Big Mac will cost you $4.19 or more, depending on the state, but in Massachusetts, it will cost you $7.09. In 1963, a roast turkey dinner, complete with sides, cost 70¢. If you bought a home as an investment property in 2008 and paid $250,000, then decided to buy one just like it today, you would need over $350,000! But if you sold the one you bought in 2008 for $350,000, you would have to pay a hefty capital gains tax, perhaps $20,000; so in real dollars, you lost money! Who gains from a cheaper dollar? Debtors do, including the big debtor, the US government. In a way, it incentivizes the government to borrow.

Who is the main player in all this? It is the Federal Reserve System, which has a dual mandate of pursuing maximum employment and price stability. The two goals are frequently contradictory (e.g., raising rates to bring down inflation will also increase unemployment and cause price instability, and the Fed is always really guessing as to what the appropriate interest rate enabling them to pursue that dual mandate is). They look at all the economic indicators—some of which are leading indicators, some coincident, and some lagging—and try to interpret them as best they can (e.g., to determine if inflation is only "transitory").

So who gets hurt by higher interest rates? Small business owners, who are 60 percent of the economy, take a direct hit; they either absorb the extra cost, pass it on to consumers, stop expanding, reduce operations and dismiss workers, or just close up shop. The government has no problem; they just print more money.

Is there an answer? Yes! Change the Fed's dual mandate to a new single mandate of pursuing a stable dollar. This can easily be done by considering the dollar's value in terms of gold or a basket of commodities, which includes gold. Let's stop the Fed from continuing to create financial havoc every few years by guessing their best trying to fulfill an impossible-to-fulfill dual mandate.

The bottom line: give the Federal Reserve Board the new single mandate of pursuing a stable dollar.

MILITARY RECRUITING

Volunteering for military duty isn't working too well; there are serious shortfalls in recruiting, questioning the sustainability of an all-volunteer force.

The fact that the military is hiring diversity, equity, and inclusion specialists at $80,000 to $180,000 a year isn't helping. It turns off any potential recruit who comes from a traditional background, does not add to combat skills, and reduces the pay of a soldier in the field. And it's paid for with your tax dollars. You can safely bet your bottom dollar that the Chinese are not spending military dollars on woke training.

The combat troops in the most efficient military forces will be all male. A year-long Marine Corps study found that all male infantry units were faster, more lethal, and more able to evacuate wounded soldiers in less time than mixed-gender test groups. Simply put, the study found that the average man was stronger than the average woman. Viewed from another angle, "every sentient adult knows what happens when you mix healthy young men and women together in small groups for extended periods of time. Just look at any workplace. Couples form. At some point, how couples interact—sexually, emotionally, happily and/or unhappily—makes life uncomfortable for those around them. Factor in intense, intimate conditions and you can forget about adults being able to stay professional 24/7."[3]

Members of Congress always seem eager to fund and extend wars that have never been declared. But perhaps seven or eight mem-

---

[3] Anna Simons, *War on the Rocks*, "Here's Why Women in Combat Units is a Bad Idea," Blogs-Charlie Mike (November 18, 2014).

bers of Congress had sons serving in Iraq—quite rare. In World War II, many members of Congress had sons involved in the fighting; it wasn't rare. Does this matter? Yes, it does; a study found that lawmakers who didn't have draft-age sons were significantly more likely to support hawkish policies over the course of World War I, World War II, the Korean War, and the Vietnam War.[4]

The answer to all this is to bring back the draft; that way, everyone's son can be drafted, and congressmen can again have "kin in the game." Another benefit to the draft is that it gives our young men a chance to serve, bond with our country, and better understand the sacrifices others have made. Democracy doesn't come free.

The bottom line: it's time to bring back the draft.

---

[4] Zaid Jilani, *The Intercept*, "'No Kin in the Game': Study Finds Members of Congress Without Draft-Age Sons Were More Hawkish" (October 11 2017).

RADIO, TV, AND CABLE

The Communications Act of 1934 gives the Federal Communications Commission exclusive jurisdiction over interstate telecommunications and information services.

If you are a broadcaster, whether radio, TV, or cable, you need a license to operate from the FCC.

Broadcasters should be held to a standard of truthfulness when it comes to the dissemination of facts (versus opinions). Loss of license should be the penalty for failure to do so. If the FCC does not currently have the authority to do this, change the law to enable this.

Fact-checkers can be the monitors.

It's in the public interest to rid ourselves of propaganda channels and ensure we have information and opinion channels.

The bottom line: broadcasters should lose their license to operate if they disseminate false information.

ELECTIONS

Try to get an appointment with a member of Congress. It's almost impossible unless you are a big donor.

We should change the rules so you can donate money to a political candidate only if you can vote for them, and only individuals should be able to donate. This would ensure that outside interests do not elect the person that represents you.

Campaigning should be limited to six months prior to an election, and as part of their FCC license, broadcasters should be obligated to host a forum or debate of candidates at least once in each of those months.

The total number of representatives in the US Congress should be increased or decreased every decade, when the census is taken, to reflect population change. One congressman today represents seven hundred thousand citizens, many more than ten years ago. In 1929, when we first had 435 congressmen, the number was three hundred thousand.

Section 230 is a provision of federal law that protects website hosts like Google and Facebook from legal liability from online information provided by third parties. The idea was to promote an unfettered community clearing house for ideas. But Section 230 also allows these website hosts to moderate content *according to their own sets of standards*, ostensibly to protect the public from "harmful content" like "hate speech," "incitement to violence," etc. But this is obviously subjective to one degree or another. Section 230 should be modified to deny liability protection for any content that is changed or blocked. This is the only way to ensure neutrality and to enable the freedom of speech guaranteed by the First Amendment. Section

230 should not be enabled, which is presently the case, to violate the First Amendment.

You should be able to vote only in person and only on election day (absentee ballots still available). When voting, it should be by paper ballot only (impossible to hack), and you should provide a photo ID. Any other system invites fraud and manipulation. It defies logic and common sense to allow someone to vote for a candidate two weeks prior to an election, and leave them in a position where they cannot change their vote because of intervening events during that two-week period.

Election day should be a national holiday. We do not need a new national holiday: combine it with an existing national holiday.

The bottom line: remove from the election process—to the extent possible—the influence of outside money, lobbying groups, and other special interests by adopting the above commonsense provisions.

SOCIAL MEDIA PLATFORMS

Section 230 (c) (1) of the 1996 Communications Decency Act protects social media platforms like Twitter (now X) and Facebook from legal liability relating to content posted on their sites by third parties. The idea was to encourage a town hall environment where anyone could freely communicate their ideas, and the host platform itself would not feel any pressure to interfere with this free exchange of ideas. The second section of the CDA, Section 203 (c) (2) allows these platforms for free speech and information to moderate content *according to their own sets of standards*. It does not require them to remove anything, but if they choose to remove "harmful content" (e.g., hate speech, sex trafficking, or incitement to violence), they are protected from liability.

When it comes to content moderation, these platforms are absolutely a black box. They have a monopoly on data and information you would need to assess whether or not there's political or other bias, and they will not give you that data and information. Their algorithms are not public information. These platforms are not operating in the legality and the spirit of the protection against liability given to them by violating the First Amendment by blocking content at the request of US government employees (e.g., the *New York Post*'s story on the Hunter Biden laptop just two weeks prior to the 2020 presidential election and numerous stories on COVID-19 shots and effective treatments).

The blocking of the Hunter Biden laptop story probably cost President Trump reelection, as polls showed that almost one in five people who voted for Biden would not have done so if aware of this story. Hydroxychloroquine was a proven and effective drug, and cheap. Yet any discussion of its effect was blocked on these platforms, and only false information about its effectiveness was allowed. Dr. Harvey Risch, a professor emeritus of epidemiology at the Yale School of Public Health, argued that the suppression of hydroxychloroquine by the Centers for Disease Control resulted in "hundreds of thousands, if not millions of deaths"!

We possibly would not have ever known about all this if Elon Musk had not bought Twitter (now X) and revealed that the government promoted suppression of facts and free speech.

What to do now? Suspicions that the social media platforms were politically biased are adequately supported in fact. Senator Ted Cruz states that these platforms know exactly how many Republicans for office had their posts blocked, and how many Democrats. It's a concrete number says the senator, but they refuse to give it.[5]

Social media platforms should not be in a position to control free speech and the free flow of ideas.

Senator Josh Hawley introduced a bill tying Section 230 protection to a new requirement that the platforms prove political neutrality every two years. The problem is that a lot of damage can be done over a two-year time period.

The bottom line: social media platforms should be given Section 230 protection only for content posted, not for content moderated or blocked.

---

5 Senator Cruz, "Zero Accountability from Big Tech Is Dangerous" (4/20/21).

SCHEDULE F

When a president is elected, he should have an opportunity to implement the policies he believes in and was elected on. Well, guess what? Part of the "deep state" or "Washington swamp" are civil servants who do not do as the president directs; they obfuscate, refuse to act, delay, modify, or even act contrary to what is requested of them by the president. And the president cannot fire them because they have civil service protection!

One cannot say that this is how democracy works best.

There is a simple answer to this. Schedule F. A section of the Civil Service Reform Act of 1978, 5 U.S.C. § 7511 (1) (2), exempts from civil service protections federal employees "whose position has been determined to be of a confidential policy-determining, policy-making or policy-advocating character."

President Donald Trump issued Executive Order 13957 on October 21, 2020, creating Schedule F in the Excepted Service that directed agencies to reclassify federal service employees in the competitive service who serve in policy-related roles as members of the excepted service.

Excepted service is a term used to refer to positions in the civil service that are specifically excluded from the requirements of the Civil Service Act.

The purpose of Executive Order 13957 was to increase flexibility in hiring and firing and to improve performance management and accountability. Civil service employees designated "Schedule F" would not be covered under the Civil Service Rules and Regulations, including due process and possibly collective bargaining rights; they would lose their employment protections upon reassignment, making them functionally at-will employees.

President Biden repealed Executive Order 13957 on his first day of office. With all the things that go through a president's mind, President Biden wasn't able to focus on improving performance management and accountability.

In case one gets the idea that, now, all civil service employees can be assigned to the excepted service and Schedule F, of the 2 million federal workers, perhaps as many as 50,000 workers could be affected.[6] So 1,950,000 workers can continue to do their jobs and enjoy full civil service protection, and the 50,000 designated Schedule F can do their jobs faithfully and dutifully or risk being replaced by someone who will.

The bottom line: designate all employees involved in confidential policy-determining, policy-making, or policy-advocating Schedule F employees.

---

[6]   Axios (July 23, 2022).

STUDENT LOANS

Let's keep it simple. President Biden decided to cancel $420 billion in federal student loan payments. He did not have the authority to do that. The budget is Congress's domain, not the president's. It's called separation of powers. The Supreme Court agreed that the president did not have the power to cancel the debt.

As far as we know, no student had a gun to his head when taking the loan. Each student had ample opportunity to investigate whether or not the course of studies the loan was taken for, when completed, would be remunerative enough to the student in the workplace to enable the student to repay the loan in a timely fashion.

But President Biden has a good heart, and wanted to help out this student, and many other students, by terminating their obligation to repay their loans.

Let's go into this a little further. Many students who took out student loans have already fully repaid them. Many other students never took out loans; just paid their tuition as they worked their way through college. Millions of other citizens never went to college. Why, under these circumstances, should all our country's taxpayers be obligated to take on an additional $420 billion in national debt? *They shouldn't!*

The school getting the loan money from the federal government should have a stake in all this, an incentive to ensure that the loan is made to the right student for the right curriculum for a predictably positive outcome. Let's say a 50 percent stake; if the student defaults, the school pays 50 percent, and the taxpayers pay 50 percent.

But why should taxpayers be on the hook at all? The school is best able to determine what curriculum will best enable the student to succeed in the marketplace, and whether that will enable the student to repay the loan. Why should taxpayers share in losses incurred by bad or unsuccessful loan decisions made by the school? *They shouldn't!*

The bottom line: get the federal government out of the student loan business, and in the interim, mandate that schools accepting the loan have some skin in the game.

FLAT TAX

In FY 2022, the IRS had 79,070 full-time equivalent positions (FTE). There's been a proposal to add eighty-seven thousand new agents. The IRS has spent $10 million on weaponry and gear since 2020.

There have been numerous reports of IRS agents coming to people's homes unannounced and knocking on the door, some not identifying themselves, and using intimidating language. How often and how true is obviously difficult to quantify.

There's a way to greatly reduce the probability of an armed IRS agent knocking on your door and intimidating you; greatly reduce the size of the IRS by greatly reducing the number of IRS agents needed, and it would save billions of dollars. We can do that by passing a flat tax.

Everyone would pay a flat tax of, say, 15 percent with no deductions, no exclusions, no exemptions, no omissions, and no credit.

> The only people who benefit from a complicated, barnacle-encrusted 70,000 page tax code are tax attorneys, accountants, lobbyists, IRS agents, and politicians who use the tax code as a way to buy and sell favors.[7]

This is basically Washington versus America, corruption in politics, and the influence of big money.

The "wealthy" <u>do</u> pay their fair share of taxes. In 2020, the top 1 percent paid 42.3 percent of the total federal income tax while

---

[7] Stephen Moore, *The Weekly Standard*.

receiving 22.2 percent of the total adjusted gross income.[8] But if you desire to make the rich pay even more, go to a Flat Tax, which eliminates the tax loopholes.

The wealthy and politically connected <u>do</u> utilize these loopholes. Well over half the money lost to loopholes comes from the top 1 percent.[7]

End the charitable deduction tax dodge and people like Bill Gates will have to pay taxes on billions of dollars of income which is not currently taxed. The Gates Foundation does support charities like Harvard University and the Sierra Club, but perhaps one can make the case that all Americans should be the charity.

The bottom line: Pass a flat tax! A flat tax is a fair tax.

---

[8] *The Hill* (March 11, 2023).

RIGHT TURNS ON RED

In 1973, the _Arab Oil Embargo_ and subsequent energy shortage prompted the federal government, as a gas-saving measure, to give states the choice of allowing right turns on red or losing federal funding. On January 1, 1980, Massachusetts was the last state to allow right turns on red.

I don't know how much gas was saved, but a 1982 study found that, in Ohio, allowing right turns on red resulted in a 57 percent increase in collisions involving right-turning vehicles and pedestrians, and an 80 percent increase involving right-turning vehicles and cyclists. In Wisconsin, the figures were 107 percent and 72 percent!

One doesn't have to go into the actual figures (which are available) to acknowledge that many pedestrians and cyclists were injured and that quite a few were killed.

The crosswalk just before the red light, where pedestrians have the right of way and are trying to cross, is frequently encroached on by the car making the right turn, while pedestrians have to wait, go around the car, or play dodge 'em.

Once the right turn is made, pedestrians in that crosswalk, who are either in the crosswalk because of a "walk" sign or because they looked to the left and right and saw no oncoming traffic, can be surprised by that car making the right turn.

The driver of the car turning right on red is multitasking; is looking to the left for traffic while also trying to keep track of pedestrians and cyclists in the crosswalk after the turn is made. Even a very diligent driver can be surprised by a pedestrian, or especially a cyclist entering that crosswalk after the turn is initiated.

Another dangerous situation arises when the driver making a right turn on red has to cross three or four lanes of traffic to make a U-turn to go in the opposite direction. With modern technology enabling more and more cars to have "auto stop," the feature that turns off the engine when the car is stopped and the driver has their foot on the brake pedal, to save gas; it is getting harder and harder to justify allowing right turns on red.

The bottom line: eliminate the legality of turning right on red.

Many municipalities have already recognized the increased danger of allowing right turns on red. Ann Arbor, Michigan, now prohibits right turns at red lights in the downtown area. New York City has long prohibited turns on red in Manhattan. The city council of Washington, DC, in 2023 approved banning right turns on red to take effect in 2025. San Francisco is entertaining the idea of a ban,[9] as is Atlanta.

---

[9] Jeff McMurray and the Associated Press, "Bicycle, Safety Advocates Nationwide Say Enough Is Enough: It's Time for Cities to Ban Right Turns on Red Lights," *Fortune*, November 4, 2023.

BALANCED BUDGET

The US Constitution does not have a balanced budget provision, and Congress rarely passes a balanced budget. Amendments to the Constitution, which would require a balanced budget, have been proposed, but none have become law. A private company must be profitable to continue to exist (i.e., revenues must exceed expenditures). The US government in a sense is a publicly held company. Because it can print money, the government can spend more than it takes in longer than a private company can, but as the debt grows, inflation and a more slowly growing economy become factors.

Inflation erodes the purchasing power of the dollar. Thanksgiving dinner in 2022 cost American families 23 percent more than it did in 2021, and the 2021 cost was 10 percent higher than the previous year. Inflation, over time, increases the price of goods and services. A Hershey individual chocolate bar with almonds cost 5¢ at the checkout counter in 1967, compared to $1.29–$1.79 today. Inflation makes it easier for the government to pay its debt (cheaper dollars), but, in a sense, incentivizes the government to continue borrowing.

The bottom line: The US Constitution should be amended to require a balanced budget. Even without an amendment, common sense and sound economics dictate that.

Very rarely can an unbalanced budget be justified (e.g., when we are at war).

COLLEGE COSTS

My eLearning, using College Board data, found 'that the average cost of going to a private college—including tuition, fees, books, and room and board—went from $2,930 in 1971 to $51,690 in 2021. That was an increase of roughly 4.6 times the rate of inflation over the past 50 years."[10]

For public colleges, the annual cost went from $1,410 to $22,690 with out-of-state students being tagged with $39,510.[10]

While student debt has continued to grow unabated according to the New York FED, US college enrollment has declined every year from 2012 to 2019, as students think twice about the cost of college and the loans that come with it.[10]

The New York Fed found that colleges raised tuition by 60 percent after an expansion in student loan credit in the 1980s. Colleges can charge what they want because the FEDS will guarantee the loan.

The bottom line: make college affordable again by removing the federal government from the student loan business.

---

[10] Breck Duma, Fox Business Economy (August 23, 2022).

REGULATIONS

Regulations, in a very real sense, are a tax.

Let's think of it this way: If you operate a business, you must follow all regulations, be they tax, health, environmental, etc. The more time you must devote to complying with regulations, the less time you can devote to growing your business, which by the way would enable you to pay more in taxes. Eventually, as more regulations are added, you have to hire another employee to keep track and comply. President Trump, on January 30, 2017, signed an executive order—Executive Order 13771—requiring that for every new federal regulation implemented, two must be rescinded, and that the net incremental cost to not exceed zero; that the cost of new regulations should be offset by the regulations being rescinded. This executive order made *common sense*, but President Biden rescinded it on January 20, 2021, his first day in office, perhaps understandably for a fellow who's never met a payroll. President Trump's EPA implemented a cost/benefit analysis rule for new environmental regulations, which has also been rescinded by President Biden. This is a regrettable rescission, which will cost taxpayers money and result in the approval of economically unsound regulations, but then again, President Biden never met a payroll; spending other people's money is not quite the same as spending your own.

The bottom line: regulations are a tax equivalent and should never be passed unless a cost/benefit analysis shows that the benefit exceeds the cost.

MARIJUANA/CANNABIS

States that have legalized recreational marijuana have had an increase in traffic crashes and deaths.

> After legalization and the launch of retail sales, there was a 5.8% rise in the incidence of traffic collision injuries and a 4.1% increase in the rate of fatal crashes, according to…analysis of five states that permit people age 21 and older to consume marijuana recreationally. In a comparative group of states without marijuana legalization, the researchers did not see any rise during the same period.[11]

More recently, the legalization of marijuana has led to a "massive increase"[12] in mental health illness, and issues like suicide and increased risk for psychosis. Cannabis has been genetically bred to be much more potent (ten to forty times more potent)[13] than previously, enabling it to quintuple your risk of psychosis and schizophrenia. The human "brain is developing until age 25 or 30," and taking cannabis "attacks the very critical centers of your brain."[12] Twenty-three states have legalized marijuana.

---

[11] Charles M. Farmer, PhD, Samuel S. Monfort, PhD, and Amber N. Woods, PhD, "Changes in Traffic Crash Rates After Legalization of Marijuana: Results by Crash Severity," *Journal of Studies on Alcohol and Drugs* (July 19, 2022).

[12] Dr. Kevin Sabet, Interview with Fox News's Trey Gowdy on *Sunday Night in America*.

[13] Eagle Forum Report, "Throwing Americans Under the Cannabis" (August 2023).

It's not necessary to criminalize marijuana, but it definitely should not be given a state's stamp of approval by legalizing and normalizing it. Legalization is followed by retail stores which increase access even more.

The bottom line: retail marijuana use should not be legal.

MENTAL ASYLUMS

> Decades ago the U.S. made a decision to end the institutionalization of all but the most dangerous mentally ill, but too many of them now wander the streets and occasionally turn violent. Several have pushed unsuspecting passengers onto the subway tracks to their deaths, in stories New Yorkers know all too well.[14]

Mental asylums, also known as insane asylums or psychiatric hospitals, housed 560,000 patients in 1955. The hospitals were massive. Wayne County's (Michigan) Eloise Psychiatric Hospital, the largest in the United States, consisted of 78 buildings on 902 pastoral acres with 10,000 patients and 2,000 staff. Eloise even had a cemetery, which meant that many of the patients were there for a lifetime. And it wasn't hard to get in. You could get institutionalized for alcoholism, dementia, depression, and epilepsy; so "insanity" in those years was broadly defined.

In the 1950s and 1960s, homelessness declined to the point that researchers were predicting its virtual disappearance in the 1970s. Today, 600,000 people are homeless in our country on an average night according to the Department of Housing and Urban Development (HUD). Forty percent of these people are unsheltered, defined by HUD as someone who lacks a fixed, regular, and adequate nighttime residence. Think of abandoned buildings, train stations, airports, camping grounds, and the streets. Twenty percent are dealing with severe mental illness. There are many sleeping in tents on

---

[14] *The Weekend Wall Street Journal*, OpEd, May 13–14, 2023.

sidewalks, defecating, urinating, and "shooting up" drugs as children walk by on the way to school.

Basically, today, the people that used to live in mental asylums now live on the streets as Eloise and other mental asylums have shut down! *Or they are in prisons*. The number of inmates in 1965 was 185,000. Today's number is 1,900,000, and it's thought that perhaps 25 percent of prison inmates have a serious mental disorder. Prisons cannot treat those with mental disorders, so the mentally ill inmate's condition can continue to deteriorate, which can create problems with other inmates.

So how did the deinstitutionalization of the mentally ill happen?

For one thing, perhaps the requirements for commitment were too broad. As noted earlier, you could get committed for alcoholism or epilepsy.

For another thing, psychiatrists in the asylums prescribed restraints, isolation, electric shock therapy, ice baths, forced drugging, and even lobotomies. This was the medical thinking at the time but this didn't pass muster as time evolved, and as public attitudes changed, the belief grew that mental hospitals were cruel and inhumane.

And finally, money. States, counties, and public entities in general had a strong desire to reduce the rising costs of mental asylums.

All this coincided with the introduction of psychotic drugs. In 1955 the drug Thorazine was introduced to treat psychotic disorders, so patients started being released from mental asylums, and they were prescribed Thorazine. It turned out that Thorazine had some serious side effects, but the exodus had started.

In 1963, President John F. Kennedy signed the Community Mental Health Act, aimed at eliminating mental asylums in favor of 1,500 local clinics where patients could receive needed drugs and therapies without institutionalization; they could be treated while working and living at home. Only half were built. They were never fully funded, and in the meantime, about 90 percent of beds were cut at state hospitals.[15] Also, the neighborhoods they were in did not

---

[15] USA Today, Patrick Kennedy, October 20, 2013.

want them. As a result, people who did need institutional care were thrown out, and there was no alternative policy in place to address their needs. The sickest people had nowhere to turn; they ended up homeless, abusing substances, or in prison. The three largest mental health providers in the nation today are jails: Cook County in Illinois, Los Angeles County in California, and Rikers Island in New York.

President Kennedy was not able to follow up with improved legislation; this was the last bill he signed before he was assassinated.

To add to the complexity of the situation, civil libertarians came to the fore, with the help of the courts. For example, a federal district court in *Lessard v. Schmidt* (1972) ruled that involuntary commitment must be limited to cases involving the "extreme likelihood" that someone "will do immediate harm to himself or others." Well, many of these people who were not deemed a threat under guidelines like these went on to commit murder, assault with intent to kill, and other crimes. Perhaps the laws should err on the side of protecting the public.

So you have people who need mental health services and cannot receive them now living on the streets and making the streets unlivable and dangerous to others, or living in prison. They are living on the streets because they are deemed to be at very low risk of becoming violent, but some of them go on to commit serious crimes.

The public has a right to clean and safe streets. Those who attest they need help by not taking their medication, by not being able to recover from their first episode of illness, by not seeking treatment from professionals, and by creating unsanitary and unhealthy conditions in the community, should be institutionalized for their sake and the community's sake.

There is also a cost to homelessness. HUD once estimated that the government spends about $40,000 per homeless person per year.[16] The state of California has spent $20 billion on homelessness since 2020. Homelessness also puts people at higher risks for

---

[16] Our Father's House Soup Kitchen, "How Homelessness Affects Society" (June 27, 2021).

victimization, poor health, loneliness, and depression. Homelessness impacts the availability of healthcare resources, crime and safety, the workforce, and the use of tax dollars.

So what is the benefit of homelessness? Nada.

The bottom line: bring back mental asylums.

THE FAA AND THE TRAINING OF AIR TRAFFIC CONTROLLERS

It's not easy to become an air traffic controller. After getting your college degree, you have to attend one of the few schools that offer certified training programs, which typically take two to four years. Then you must do well on an eight-hour exam which is comprised of "seven cognitive tests to measure the right aptitudes required for a career in air traffic control". Unlike your standard final exam, there's no studying for this aptitude evaluation.

> *The only way you pass this test is if you've been paying close attention to the past few years of training.*[17] (emphasis added)

It's a stressful job, perhaps confirmed by the mandatory retirement age of fifty-five.

In the news recently have been stories of taxiing airliners crossing an active runway, airliners instructed to land on an occupied runway, flights scrubbed or delayed because air traffic control centers had shut down because of a shortage of controllers, and other anomalies.

You would think that the Federal Aviation Administration would think of ways to incentivize people to become controllers. You would be wrong. In December 2013, the Obama administration scrapped much of the training program, including the aptitude test,

---

[17] Mountain States Legal Foundation MSLF The Litigator Vol. 2, "PULLING THE RUG – When Ideology Trumps Merit" (2023).

in favor of a "biographical questionnaire" in an effort to "diversify" the federal government—diversity over merit.

On April 11, 2013, a young American by the name of Matthew Douglas scored a perfect 100 on the aptitude test. Matthew also graduated early with a 4.0 GPA. The new test "asked questions about his favorite and worst subjects in high school, what sports he enjoyed, how friends might describe him, or if he'd ever been unemployed."[18]

Matthew was rejected for being "biographically ineligible."

What a mess! Now the public and pilots don't know if the controller directing their flight is there because of ability or because of "diversity preference."

What's the incentive for somebody to attend four years of college and two to four more years of specialized training, not knowing if your best efforts and top grades mean anything? How does the guy feel who knows he got a job he didn't deserve to get?

Perhaps the Supreme Court decision in *Students for Fair Admissions v. Harvard*, which took away the legality of affirmative action, will settle the matter.

One possible solution to the controller shortage would be for the government to pay half the tuition every semester for a student enrolled in a certified training program, at semester's end, if a score of, say, 3.0 or higher was achieved. Repeat every semester. When the student graduates and achieves a score of, say, 70 or higher on the aptitude exam, he is fully reimbursed for the other half of the tuition. This can continue until the FAA is fully staffed.

When we look to the skies, we should see blue, not bias.

The bottom line: the public interest and the candidates' interest require that air traffic controller hiring should be strictly merit-based.

---

[18] Ibid.

PLASTIC IN OUR FOOD

For the Fourth of July, we enjoyed a family meal featuring wild-caught Alaska sockeye salmon. Wild salmon is more nutritional than farm-raised salmon and has higher amounts of natural minerals, including calcium and iron. Additionally, farmed salmon has triple the fat content of wild-caught salmon. *But both wild-caught and farmed salmon contain microplastics*—small particles of plastic.

Where do microplastics and the even smaller in size nanoplastics come from? Some of these particles come from plastic grocery bags. Of single-use grocery bags, only 1 percent are recycled.[19] If not recycled or deposited in a garbage dump, they float around freely by highways and byways until they find their way to a drain or creek or river leading eventually to the ocean, or are thrown into the ocean directly, either accidentally or purposefully, perhaps from boating activities.

A plastic bag can just float in the ocean, at least for a while; a plastic bag was found at a depth of thirty-six thousand feet in the Mariana Trench! The bag, as it's tossed around in the ocean, can break apart eventually into small pieces called microplastics, or even smaller pieces called nanoplastics. The plastic is always in the water, in one size or another, as it can take three hundred to one thousand years for the plastic to decompose. Because it takes so long for plastic bags to disintegrate, they can be ingested by whales, dolphins, and other sea creatures. This blocks their digestive systems and results in death.

How does the plastic get into our food supply? Zooplankton and other small marine creatures eat phytoplankton laden with

---

[19] The World Counts.

microplastics and nanoplastics, which then become food for fish. The bigger fish like salmon eat the smaller fish, and eventually we eat the salmon.

At a recent visit to a grocery store, there was the typical carousel with spokes at the end of the checkout counter. A clerk placed my purchases in several single-use plastic bags hanging on several spokes of the carousel. I never intended to eat the plastic.

The bottom line: ban single-use plastic bags!

THE DEPARTMENT OF EDUCATION (DOE)

The US Congress passed legislation to create the first DOE in 1867. President Andrew Jackson signed that legislation. The first commissioner was given a staff of three and two rooms. It was a non-cabinet level agency, whose mission was to collect information (information data, research, best practices), and statistics about the nation's schools and improve national education by disseminating that information to local and state-level authorities.

Due to concerns however, that the DOE *would exercise too much control over local schools*, the new department was demoted to an Office of Education in 1868.

Let's fast forward to 1979. On October 17 of that year, the DOE was resurrected. In his State of the Union Speech in 1982, President Ronald Reagan[20] called for an end to the DOE. His belief was that *decisions about education should be made at the local level*. President Reagan failed in his effort to abolish the DOE. Today's DOE has 4,400 employees and a budget of $68 billion.

The DOE provides money to colleges and universities among other entities, but they can attach strings to those funds.

If a school accepts funds, it is subject to Title IX, which is a civil rights law (enforced by the DOE's Office for Civil Rights) to prohibit "sex-based discrimination (in other words, sexual harassment) in any school or any other education program that receives fund-

---

[20] During his 1980 presidential campaign, President Reagan vowed to eliminate the DOE.

ing from the federal government."[21] Sexual harassment is any sexual activity or act (including rape, but also unwanted touching) that happens without consent. Students must be able to avail themselves of the protections afforded under Title IX by contacting a Title IX coordinator by mail, electronic mail, or in person. The coordinator must be a full-time position, which of course involves a salary, and likely the salary of supporting staff. This obviously does not make the student's cost of education cheaper. For quite a while, the guidelines allowed a female student to file a rape complaint and not even have to face the male defendant in a hearing (Betsy DeVos, when she was DOE's Secretary, changed the policy to allow students to question one another during live hearings), and after the hearing, police were occasionally called in, and still are.

If schools do not accept federal funds, they are not subject to Title IX. Since all public schools receive federal funding, only private schools (like Hillsdale College) can refuse, by not accepting federal funds, to be dragged into adjudicating complaints of sexual harassment, rape, etc. Why can't local police departments, or the school itself, handle these complaints without federal involvement? *They can.*

The bottom line: Education should be local. Make it local again by eliminating the Department of Education.

---

[21] Wikipedia.

SOCIAL SECURITY

The Social Security system will run out of money in the next ten to twelve years. The insolvency date can be delayed if the retirement age is raised from the current sixty-seven years of age to seventy. If nothing is done, when insolvency happens, benefit payments will be reduced.

The funds Social Security receives are invested in US Treasury securities, like Treasury bills, (maximum one-year maturity) notes (two- to ten-year maturities), and bonds (twenty- or thirty-year maturities). The government can also borrow surplus funds from the Social Security trust fund and pay interest on the funds borrowed. In 2021, the 2.9 trillion dollars in the Trust Fund earned 1.4 percent. In 2021, the Standard & Poor 500, a stock index of the five hundred largest US companies, was up 26.89 percent. In measuring the returns of stocks and bonds from 1928 through 2021, the Federal Reserve Bank of St. Louis found that stocks returned 11.82 percent a year, T-bills 3.33 percent a year, and T-bonds 5.11 percent a year. $100 invested in stocks (S&P 500) grew to about $761,710 by the end of 2021 while $100 invested in T-bills grew to about $2,083 and $100 in T-bonds grew to about $8,526.

It would not be prudent to invest all Social Security Trust funds in stocks because there are years in which stocks are sharply down in value while bonds are up. But it certainly makes sense to invest some of the funds in stocks (e.g., 30 percent to 50 percent) in an attempt to delay or eliminate insolvency.

President George W. Bush proposed and strongly campaigned for a voluntary personal account option where part of one's Social Security taxes would be invested in a personal Social Security account. Because the funds would be invested in a conservative mix of stock and bond funds, the returns of a personal account would have the opportunity to be much higher than the returns of the Social Security Trust itself. The personal account, in addition to providing the opportunity for higher returns, allows for the owner to pass along the account to his children, and would not be affected by an insolvency in the Social Security Trust fund.

The bottom line: invest some of the Social Security trust funds in stock funds and create the option for personal Social Security accounts.

SAVING WATER

When you turn on your water faucet, it's not unusual to have to wait thirty seconds or even forty-five or sixty seconds to get warm water. The way we heat water is absolutely wasteful; millions of gallons of a valuable resource go right down the drain. In a state like Florida (and thirteen other states), we are facing a "high risk" of water shortages by the year 2050 according to a study by the Natural Resources Defense Council.

There's a simple and good solution! It's called a tankless water heater (there is no water tank; water is heated as it passes through the pipes). It is more compact than a hot water tank, and you'll never have water leaking all over your floor or basement.

It still may take fifteen seconds or so to get warm water, unless your unit also has a recirculation pump, which takes care of that problem.

It gets even better. If your unit has condensing capability, which enables the unit to extract heat from the exhaust before releasing it into the venting system. This additional way to heat the water is obviously more efficient, which means that the cost of energy (either natural gas, electricity, or propane) for running the water heater is reduced. Depending on exactly what you install, you can reduce the fuel costs of heating your water by 25 percent to 50 percent! So tankless water heaters are both *fuel-efficient* and *water-efficient*!

Units with condensing capability are considered so efficient that they are certified by the federal Energy Star program, making them eligible for utility rebates.

Here's a situation where the cost/benefit analysis is easily quantifiable, and the benefit easily and hugely exceeds the cost. Do you think this is a case where the federal government can incentivize their installation by offering a tax credit for installing a tankless water heater?

The bottom line: to save energy and preserve water, the federal government should offer tax credits for the installation of tankless water heaters.

LAWYERS

What do two Americans say after they greet each other at a foreign airport? Answer: "I'll sue you!"

There is no question that America is a litigious society. How did we get there? What are the factors?

Well, one factor is lawyer advertising, which was prohibited in the United States until 1977. The concern was for the heavy losses that could be inflicted in a lawsuit, and that cases could be brought where there was no basis for a claim. But in that year, the Supreme Court of the United States overturned the prohibition[22] on free speech grounds, stating that the State Bar of Arizona "inhibited the free flow of information and kept the public in ignorance", by banning lawyer advertising.

After Bates, significant money flowed into advertising. In the top seventy-five television markets, two thousand lawyers spent almost $200,000,000 on advertising. It's estimated that 75 percent of all firms advertise.[23]

The positive about such advertising is that it makes the public aware of current legal issues and lets people know where to get legal help on these issues. The negative is that it encourages lawsuits where there really is no basis for a claim.

Another factor is the huge increase in the number of lawyers; there were 326,000 lawyers in the United States in 1970, but that number exploded to 1,327,010 active lawyers as of January 1, 2022.

Still, another factor is contingent fee lawsuits, where an attorney accepts no money for his services unless he prevails in a case, and

---

²² *Bates v. State Bar of Arizona.*
²³ Wikipedia, "Legal Advertising in the United States."

then he might get 30 percent to 40 percent of the settlement as payment. The positive here is that a plaintiff with no money to pursue a just cause has the ability to do so. The negative is that it could cost the plaintiff much more than standard hourly rates, and that again, it might encourage lawsuits where there is really no basis for a claim.

A final factor is class action lawsuits, where one or more plaintiffs bring a lawsuit on behalf of a larger group, known as the class, and any proceeds are shared among all members of the class. The positives here are that class action promotes judicial efficiency (e.g., 250,000 plaintiffs can be represented in one lawsuit), and it's effective for small claims where it's cost or time-prohibitive to pursue on an individual basis. The negatives are that your compensation is limited and you do not have control over the lawsuit. And the lawyers' fees are hefty (e.g., 25 percent to 33 percent of the amount of damages).

According to NERA Economic Consulting, class action settlements in recent years have averaged $56.5 million, but individual class members rarely see a fat payday. Target Corporation's computers were hacked in 2013 resulting in fraudulent charges on many of the forty million credit and debit cards that were compromised. In the proposed settlement that resulted, the plaintiffs involved would receive $10 million. If all forty million filed as plaintiffs, they could receive just 25¢ (assuming none of them could document their financial losses). The separate lawyers' fees totaled $6.75 million! I have no idea how representative this case is, but might it be more equitable to have the attorneys document their hourly time spent at, perhaps 50 percent higher than their normal rate, to compensate them for the uncertainty involved, and if that invoice totals 30 percent of the settlement or higher, allow the attorneys to receive that as a maximum payout?

In 2016, $429 billion or 2.3 percent of US gross domestic product was spent on litigation costs. The probability is that the amount is much higher today. That's a lot of GDP going to non-productive uses. How do we fix it? Even if there's a tweak that works regarding contingent fees and class action lawsuits, it might not pass constitutional muster. And even if it does, when you tweak or bend something, something else might unexpectedly break.

There is a simple solution out there if the objective is to reduce litigation and have less of our GDP spent on litigation costs and going to more productive uses, and that is:

The bottom line: make the plaintiff pay the defendant's court costs if the plaintiff loses, and this includes government plaintiffs.

ELECTRIC VEHICLES

When Henry Ford introduced his Model T automobile to the world in 1908, the buyers of his car were not incentivized by the government in any way. The world was ready for a vehicle that was affordable, durable, and simple to operate that didn't leave a lot of poop behind. It was a classic example of the free market at work; a product was introduced that filled a need and that people wanted to buy. When innovation and demand naturally intersect, you have a superior product.

Now here comes the electric vehicle. If you replace your two gas-powered cars with electric vehicles, you will now use 40 percent more electricity every month. Already California has rolling blackouts and urges residents at times to conserve energy use by raising their thermostats in the afternoon and evening hours. Yet in 2022, the California Air Resources Board set a goal that all new cars and light trucks sold in the state be electric by 2035, and the same board said that it could mean twelve million more EVs on California's roads.

Now there are many interesting items here worth mentioning. There was obviously no cost/benefit analysis done here; there are so many variables that are hard to define and quantify that you cannot do an honest one. The public wasn't clamoring for electric vehicles, so demand had to be boosted artificially by providing government incentives; there's a $7,500 tax incentive in 2024. Government bureaucrats, many of them unelected, are taking away consumer choice, basically canceling free market choice and making gasoline-powered cars increasingly more expensive as automobile companies are saddled with the huge costs involved in converting to electric vehicle production. This is central planning, not free market innovation and incentivization. Many communist and authoritarian regimes who tried this approach have proven it doesn't work. By the way, 56 percent of the lithium batteries in EVs come from China. What if a new technology proves superior, like hydrogen fuel cell-powered cars, or cars powered with mini nuclear reactors? In 1957, Ford came out with a concept car called the Nucleon, designed to be powered by a mini nuclear reactor. It wasn't feasible then, but technology advances exponentially. Is it not better to allow the free market to govern the demise of the gas-powered car?

Central planning may be failing again. A new report by the Manhattan Institute authored by Mark Mills titled "Electric Vehicles for Everyone? The Impossible Dream", concluded that "overall, the rapid electrification of the U.S. transportation sector would increase consumer costs, make the electric grid more vulnerable to blackouts, threaten national security and may not even lead to fewer greenhouse gas emissions.[24]

In another vein, the range of EVs is problematic, and their range is even worse in cold and hot temperatures. Batteries catch fire and explode. The government did not help Henry Ford by funding the building of gas stations, but it is helping EV manufacturers, with public funds, in the building of charging stations. Henry Ford's Model T was a free-market winner, let's allow EVs to show if they can be a free-market winner.

Regulating EVs into dominance, or any product, is what command economies in the past have tried unsuccessfully to do. That approach stifles innovation, misallocates public resources, and might even mean that fossil fuel-powered vehicles will be around longer if that is considered a negative. I wonder if the California Air Resources Board has a card up its sleeve. After all, they are very smart people, although I don't know how many of their people have ever met a payroll. It's possible that, if their religious advocacy of EVs fails, they will propose elevated highways so you are always going downhill. Think of all the electricity that would save!

---

[24] Fox News.com/Thomas Catenacci/July 18, 2023.

The bottom line: Stop the government from subsidizing and advocating for EVS and from advocating against gas-powered vehicles. The free market is the most efficient vehicle for making these decisions.

THE SOUTHERN BORDER

If you are a citizen of another country and live abroad, it can take you seven to thirty-three months to get a green card, which allows you to live permanently in the United States.

Six million people apply for green cards every year, and about one million receive a green card every year. Thousands of green card applications are denied every year.

But why bother to invest all this time to come to the US legally; just go to Mexico and walk across the southern border. We can then call you an illegal immigrant because you just violated US immigration rules and regulations. Someone who enters our country illegally is subject to detainment and deportation at any time. But that's not what happens. The migrants have been coached to seek asylum on the basis of being persecuted in their own country.

In reality, they are not fleeing persecution, but seeking economic opportunity.

Unfortunately, the people currently in charge of our immigration system, who swore with their hand on the Bible to uphold the laws of the United States, have decided to do otherwise; they've decided that they are the law. Hence, the present situation.

Instead of being detained and turned back, they are given food, shelter, medical care, and transportation to anywhere in the United States they choose to go to, all at taxpayer expense, which the taxpayers never voted on. The state they go to might even give them a driver's license.

They are given immigration court dates, which can be set as late as 2032 or even 2035; and in the meantime, they can receive a work permit and legally live and work in the US until their court date comes up. Many do not show up for their court hearings.

It takes from ninety minutes to two hours to process the illegal immigrant. Sometimes Immigration and Customs Enforcement (ICE) is so overwhelmed that they just release people they have not processed into the interior with a directive to report to an ICE office within sixty days. There were 2.4 no-shows for everyone who checked in.[25] Another source says that just 13 percent show up. From mid-March to mid-July of 2021, there were fifty thousand illegals released into the US with no court date.

In the fiscal year 2022, ending September 30, 2022, 2.76 million illegal immigrants crossed our southern border with Mexico, breaking the previous annual record by more than 1 million! They cross the border and apply for asylum. That is not counting the "gotaways."

In a single week at the border, there were 50,000 Border Patrol apprehensions and over 18,600 *known* "gotaways."[26] According to CBP, more than 1.5 million "gotaways" have crossed the southern border under the Biden Administration.[27] The country they came from has no database on them, so basically we are releasing someone we don't know anything about into our country. No doubt some are criminals, gang members, drug peddlers, and sex traffickers. Common sense tells us that the percentage probably rises, perhaps exponentially, among the "gotaways."

In the first three months of fiscal year 2022, TSA allowed nearly forty-five thousand illegal immigrants to use immigration enforcement documents, like arrest warrants, as alternate forms of ID to fly within the United States.[28] As a US citizen, try showing up at an airport ticket counter with only an arrest warrant to board a flight.

In a new wrinkle, from October 2021 to February 2022, 421 illegal immigrants from China crossed our southern border without authorization; but from October 2022 to February 2023, that number increased to 4,366.[29] The number of illegals from China

---

25 Stef W. Kight, Politics & Policy, Axios (July 27, 2021).

26 Maria Bartiromo, Sunday Morning Futures on Fox News, May 6, 2023.

27 Fox News/Patrick Hauf/May 16, 2023.

28 US Senator James Risch's E-Newsletter, March 23, 2022.

29 US Customs & Border Protection.

increased drastically in fiscal year 2023 (ending September 31) to 24,341 overall encounters with 21,003 of them being single adults.[30] Any spies or saboteurs there?

Drugs come with massive and uncontrolled illegal immigration. Ninety percent of fentanyl flows through our southern border.

The people coming in do not speak our language and do not know our culture. They have to accept any wages offered and wind up taking jobs away from labor unions and low-income Americans, very much hurting the black community. For any jobs Americans don't want to fill or can't fill, issue temporary work visas, requested by prospective employers.

Some say we need more people. Well, the population of our country in 1946, after the end of World War II, was 141.39 million.

Today's population is 331.9 million. It seems like lots of people outside our country will do anything to live in our country. If the population of 2.76 million people who entered our country illegally in 2022 grows at 20 percent annually, compounded, you have over 105 million new residents in 20 years. And how many illegals will arrive each year over the next twenty years? I personally prefer more wide open spaces and crime-free cities that are easy to navigate.

The bottom line: close the southern border to illegal immigration.

---

[30] Fox News/Senator Roger Marshall/Sunday, Dec. 10, 2023

WIND AND SOLAR

If you harm in any way an American Bald Eagle (*don't pull a souvenir feather off a nesting eagle!*), you can be fined up to $5,000 or one year imprisonment, with $10,000 or not more than two years in prison for a second conviction. Felony convictions carry a maximum fine of $250,000 or two years of imprisonment. If wind turbines do not kill thousands of American Bald Eagles each year, there's no doubt that they at least kill hundreds. But it's not just eagles, in 2012, with far fewer wind turbines (wind turbines have grown fifty-sixfold over the last two decades)[31] in existence than today it is estimated that 366,000 birds were killed by turbines: eagles, migratory birds, bats (important pollinators) and others. So 8 percent to 10 percent of American power is provided by wind in a rather inefficient way; storage batteries vary in efficiency, you have to build high voltage transmission lines, and the wind doesn't always blow, plus wind turbines are unsightly, and you don't want to sleep near the whirring noises.

Then we have solar panel farms, where the space required can have a huge ecological cost to the environment, including loss of habitat and interference with rainfall and drainage, which can adversely affect native vegetation and wildlife.

Seventy-five percent of our solar panels come from *China*. In 2022, China issued permits for two new coal power plants per week.[32]

How do all these wind farms and solar panel farms get financed? Well, they are not profitable; you can't make a buck investing in these projects. In fact, you'll lose it, so the people promoting these projects

---

[31] Amy Joi O'Donaghue, "The Wicked Story of 'Clean' Wind Energy and Raptors," *Deseret News* (July 28, 2022).

[32] CREA (Center for Research on Energy and Clean Air), February 27, 2023.

don't even ask you, they ask the US government. Some people in our government even believe in Modern Monetary Theory (MMT), which suggests that the government could simply create more money without consequence as it's the issuer of the currency. Voila! The magic elixir! No need to pay anything back; just print more money! So the people who want to start wind and solar panel farms go to donor cocktail party fundraisers for politicians and donate money to them, then the politicians, to promote "green energy" of course, invest public funds into these projects. The people who run these projects make a hefty salary.

Is there a better way? Yes. Replace wind and solar panel farms with natural gas and nuclear energy.

China is using coal as a bridge to nuclear. A nuclear power plant has started operating in China using fourth-generation reactors, whereas Western countries won't have such plants online until the early 2030s. China currently operates fifty-five reactors and is now building twenty-two of the fifty-eight reactors under construction around the world.[33]

Wind farms require up to 360 times as much land to produce the same amount of electricity as a one-thousand-megawatt nuclear energy facility, solar panel farms require 75 times as much land! Nuclear plants are carbon emission-free.

Natural gas, currently classified as a dirty fuel, is relatively clean burning compared to other fossil fuels such as coal or petroleum products. We have an abundance of natural gas in our country. In fact, we liquefy it and ship it to Europe (64 percent of US LNG exports in 2022), China, and other countries. Europe has reclassified natural gas as a clean-burning fuel. Why can't we do the same in the US? We should. Former Texas governor and former US secretary of energy Rick Perry, has advocated using natural gas as a "bridge fuel" because right now we are taking fossil fuel-produced electricity off the electrical grid faster than it is being replaced with renewable energy, this while the electrical base load is increasing, base load

---

[33] Wall Street journal/Atomic Power Is In Again and China Has The Edge/by Sha Hua/12-07-2023

being defined as the minimum amount of electric power delivered or required over a given period of time at a steady rate. Perhaps we can use natural gas as a "bridge fuel" to nuclear, as it takes a while to build a nuclear reactor.

Let's stop the massive misallocation of public funds and resources by first stopping subsidizing electric vehicles. Americans on the lower end of the income pole cannot afford them, and automakers have to raise the cost of their gas-powered cars to cover losses incurred in the manufacture of electric vehicles. And we don't even know if electric vehicles can be the solution in the long run; another technology might prove to be a better answer. So the demand for electric vehicles is in a sense artificial; dictated by government mandates and incentives. Command economies are no match for free markets. But even if we assume that electric vehicles are the long-term answer, we will need nuclear power plants. Massive increases in our electrical base load will be needed. For starters, replacing your two gas-powered vehicles with EVs increases your household electrical usage by 40 percent! Assuming that 28.3 million electric vehicles will be on US roads in 2030, we will need 2.13 million level 2 and 172,000 level 3 public chargers, in addition to the units that consumers install in their own garages. McKinsey & Company's prediction is that we will need about 28 million ports by 2030.[34] As of November 8, 2022, we have 56,256 EV charging stations. Today we have 6.8 million electric vehicles on the road. There is no way we can add enough solar panel farms and wind turbine farms to provide the increase in base load needed; we will just be wasting more trillions.

The bottom line: abandon the subsidy of electric vehicles, reclassify natural gas as a clean-burning fuel, and go nuclear as rapidly as possible.

---

[34] Fox News/Opinion by Liz Peek/12-12-2023

BIRTHRIGHT CITIZENSHIP

People born on US territory are guaranteed citizenship (right of birth) (*jus soli*, "right of the soil") by the first part of the Citizenship Clause introduced by the Fourteenth Amendment to the United States Constitution (adopted July 9, 1868): "All persons born or naturalized in the United States, and subject to the jurisdiction thereof, are citizens of the United States and of the State wherein they reside."

The amendment overrode the Supreme Court decision in *Dred Scott v. Sanford* (1857) that denied US citizenship to African Americans, whether born in the United States or not and whether a slave or a free person.

If an objective was to protect slaves brought to the United States against their will who subsequently had children here; it has certainly metastasized far beyond that. The Pew Hispanic Center estimates that approximately 7.5 percent of all births in the US (about 300,000 per year) are to illegal aliens and that there are 4.5 million children born to illegal aliens who received citizenship by birth.

Birthright Citizenship has spawned "birth tourism," where pregnant women come to the United States late in their pregnancy (e.g., from *China*) to obtain citizenship for their child. Such a child is called an anchor baby if the child's citizenship is intended to help the parents obtain permanent residency.

One exception to jus soli is children born in the United States to foreign heads of state or foreign diplomats, a rather small number.

Births of illegal immigrant children will probably increase substantially because of the huge increase in illegal immigrants pouring across our southern border. For fiscal year 2022, the twelve months ending in September 2022, more than 2.76 million illegal immigrants crossed our southern border, breaking the previous annual record by more than 1 million! This number does not include the "gotaways"—those that came across by eluding any contact with the Border Patrol.

Does the Fourteenth Amendment guarantee citizenship to children of illegal immigrants? The federal courts have not come around to the idea that it doesn't. Perhaps when we consider the equity of the matter, a federal court might find it inequitable for a person who broke our laws by entering our country illegally to be rewarded by having his children born here awarded American citizenship. Barring a judicial resolution, the only other one is amending the Fourteenth Amendment, something that will probably be very difficult to accomplish.

The bottom line: stop rewarding the felony called "unlawful entry" by disallowing American citizenship to children of illegal immigrants.

ENDLESS WARS

What do the wars in *Korea, Vietnam, Iraq I, Iraq II, Afghanistan* and *Ukraine* have in common? They were never declared wars by Congress! A total of 58,220 American soldiers died in Vietnam in an undeclared war sometimes called a "police action." The last declared war was WWII, which was perhaps the last war you could justify participation in. Yet here we are again today, fighting a proxy war with Russia in Ukraine, which no US citizen voted for, which has cost us $135 billion so far, and which—if it keeps escalating—could lead to a nuclear confrontation.

Only Congress can declare war, and the War Powers Resolution of 1973 restricted the President's power to initiate war. The Resolution's Goal was to avoid long confrontations like *Vietnam*. The WPR stipulates that presidents are required to end foreign military actions after 60 days unless Congress provides a declaration of war or authorization for the operation to continue.

Is our involvement in Ukraine a "foreign military action"? You can certainly argue that having advisors on the ground in Ukraine, training their armed forces, supplying them with arms, and keeping them afloat financially qualifies as that. But it really doesn't matter if it is or it isn't since Congress has authorized it.

So the WPR did not succeed in keeping us out of another protracted war. Hundreds of thousands have been killed, millions have fled never to return, there has been vast destruction of infrastructure and the food supply, and the escalation continues toward a nuclear confrontation, not to mention $135 billion and counting. Cyprus's border has been violated since 1974 when Turkey invaded and grabbed a third of the island, and Turkey is still there, and Turkey is in the Mediterranean, an area strategically important to us. Perhaps six million people have poured over our southern border over the last three or four years, so our southern border is not inviolate but Ukraine's is?

The bottom line: amend the war powers resolution to give the American people a vote after ninety days via a national referendum on any matter where we are involved directly or indirectly in hostilities in a foreign land.

CREDIT CARD INTEREST RATE CHARGES

Credit card interest rate charges today have reached 22 percent! Not usurious, according to the present law! There are usury laws in every state that place a limit on how much a bank can charge consumers. In South Carolina, PE, it is 8.75 percent; but credit cards can charge 18 percent. Usury laws generally apply to consumer loans rather than commercial loans, so the meager protection they provide isn't available to small companies. State usury laws often don't apply to credit card loans or a national bank, and when they do, the credit card company can charge the highest interest rate allowed in the bank's home state, not the cardholder's.

The rationale for usury laws is to allow lenders to make a reasonable profit but to prevent them from imposing unreasonable or predatory interest rates. But at 22 percent, what you owe, if not paid down at all, doubles in 3.28 years! One source states that the general usury limit is 24 percent or four points above the average prime loan rate (8.5 percent today), whichever is less. Nice thought, but it can't be the case, otherwise the credit card company couldn't charge more than 12.5 percent in the present environment. But perhaps a good idea emanates from all this: that the interest rate that credit card companies charge *should* be capped at 4 percent over the prime rate. A well-managed credit card company or national bank should be able to earn a reasonable profit in this scenario without placing people in untenable financial squeezes. If you are charging 22 percent, tighten your lending standards so you can lower that rate; be more discriminating as to whom you give credit to and in determining how much credit to extend. Twenty-two percent supports a lot of deadbeats. For comparison, today's federal funds rate is 5.5 percent, the prime rate is 8.5 percent, and thirty-year mortgages are 7.5 percent. How do you justify 22 percent? You cannot.

Credit cards in your pocket incentivize impulse buying. If you go out every day with only cash in your pocket, you're much more likely to buy only things you need, rather than things you want. My high school economics teacher, Mr. Harold Mohr, and his wife got a credit card from a major department store when the store first offered it and credit cards were new. They found that they used the credit card much more than they needed to. So Mr. Mohr's advice was to follow his example, which was to freeze your credit card in a block of ice and place it in your freezer and melt down the block of ice to access your credit card only when absolutely necessary.

Most people will not follow Mr. Mohr's example, so they are still incentivized to use their credit cards to buy things they don't need and then pay exorbitant and punitive interest rates on unpaid balances. The rates are so high that they are a hindrance to consumer financial well-being, not a help.

The bottom line: cap what credit card companies and national banks can charge credit card holders at 4 percent over the prime rate.

ESG — ENVIRONMENTAL, SOCIAL, AND CORPORATE GOVERNANCE INVESTING

It wasn't too long ago that parents, schools, and religious institutions were entrusted with inculcating children with a sense of duty to society and others, and a sense of moral responsibility.

That is evidently no longer sufficient; the fad of the day is ESG.

Perhaps the most logical reason to avoid ESG is that there are no clear standards.

> The Securities and Exchange (SEC) regulates reporting for publicly traded companies. While the SEC requires companies to report certain metrics, its governance of ESG metrics is loose. As a result, every company manages its own ESG reporting.[35]

In the same vein, ESG criteria established at one institution for their index or funds have little or no bearing on the ESG criteria employed by another firm.[36] The obvious problem is that words like *environmental, social, and corporate governance* cannot be quantified; if you ask ten different people to define these terms, you'll likely get ten different answers.

---

[35] Hannah Rounds, "Pros and Cons of ESG Investing," The College Investor, Updated July 21, 2022.

[36] Kenny Zhu, SoFi LEARN, March 14, 2023.

Proponents of ESG investing claim that in addition to encouraging laudable goals (i.e., pressuring companies to consider ESG criteria in their management decisions), it enhances profits and returns. *It does not!*[37] One can argue whether or not ESG investing is a good thing or not, but it does not enhance returns; companies that focus on profits only (which is their fiduciary duty) outperform companies that don't. Dual mandates dilute focus and, in the real world, can sometimes cancel each other out (e.g., "This investment is a great one from an ESG perspective, but its profit potential is not good," or, "This investment can make us a great profit but may be dubious from an ESG perspective"). You do not want to allow company management to be able to give excuses for poor performance.

Circling back to performance, the highest-rated funds in terms of sustainability do not outperform the lowest-rated funds.[38] In 2021, while the S&P 500 was +28.41 percent with dividends reinvested, oil was +55.01 percent but was excluded from ESG portfolios. And you can get some seeming oddities like Tesla receiving a score of 37 out of 100 while Philip Morris received 84![39]

Companies in ESG portfolios have worse compliance records for both labor and environmental rules than companies in non-ESG portfolios. Why? Perhaps company management, whether they focus on ESG or not, focuses on environmental, community, customer, and employee interests anyway to maximize the company's profit potential; it's good business.

Fiduciarily, why, when we become owners of a mutual fund or other investment vehicle, can the mutual fund assume, without asking us, that they can vote our shares of the companies the mutual fund owns according to the mutual fund's interpretation of their own ESG guidelines? Do Blackrock, State Street, Vanguard, and other investment companies have a right, without the shareowner's consent, to say to a company we won't buy your shares unless you're

---

[37] Mike Edleson and Andy Puzder, "Is ESG Profitable? The Numbers Don't Lie," *The Weekend Wall Street Journal*, Sat–Sun (March 11–12, 2023).

[38] Sanjai Bhagat, "An Inconvenient Truth About Investing," *Harvard Business Review* (March 31, 2022).

[39] Shannon Thaler, *New York Post*, Business, June 15, 2023.

woke? *They do not.* As an aside, you can also make a case for companies offering non-ESG portfolios.

Blackrock, bowing to political pressure—perhaps sensing legal liability and losing a lot of business from state pension funds which are fiduciarily required to maximize returns—is starting to give investors a choice.[40] And last June, Blackrock CEO Larry Fink said he would stop using "the word ESG anymore because it's been entirely weaponized."

Finally, if you compare one company's ESG score to another company's ESG score, you may not be making relevant comparisons; you may not be comparing apples to apples.

The bottom line: ESG investing is ill-defined, costs investors their money, and makes investment decisions without shareholder input. It's the fad of the times. Avoid ESG investing.

---

[40] Salim Ramji and Joud Abdel Majeid, "BlackRock Gives Investors a Say," August 3, 2023.

MINIMUM WAGE

Many states have minimum wage laws. In Michigan, PE, the Michigan Workforce Opportunity Wage Act (WOWA) establishes the minimum wage that Michigan workers must be paid, which is currently $10.33 an hour. Overtime must be paid to someone working over forty hours in a single workweek.

Federally, minimum wage provisions are contained in the Fair Labor Standards Act (FLSA). The federal minimum wage is currently $7.25 per hour.

Five states have not adopted a state minimum wage.

Employers must meet both state and federal standards.

Minimum wage laws basically interfere with the marketplace and free market forces. Unfettered, an employee will accept the highest amount an employer is willing and able to pay. If an employer doesn't have to pay more than $10/hour to attract an employee to a particular position, why should a law dictate $17? *It should not.* Many of the politicians passing these laws do not have an economics degree, and, much more importantly, have never met a payroll. When you own a business, and, among other things, you have to meet payroll, it gives you a much better perspective on how to run a business in a way where you can better serve the public and still make a profit. You are immersed in the real world. *One of the things to look for in the resume of a person running for office is whether or not they've ever met a payroll.*

To complicate matters even more, many cities and counties in California and other states have local minimum wage laws. Perhaps local minimum wage laws make more sense than statewide laws; should the minimum wage be the same in Los Angeles and Eureka?

California also adjusts the wage annually referenced to the Consumer Price Index for urban wage earners and clerical workers.

So should the Michigan minimum wage in Ann Arbor be the same as the minimum wage in Grand Rapids? The cost of living is much higher in Ann Arbor, yet the minimum wage is the same for both cities. In the same vein, should the federal minimum wage be the same in New York City as the minimum wage in Elkhart, Indiana? Obviously not; it just makes no common sense. Politicians get together and enact laws that pass no cost/benefit analysis and can distort local economies and create unnecessary problems for local businesses.

These politicians make minimum wage laws a political football to kick around during every election cycle, preening to their constituents that they are fighting for them by supporting a hike in the minimum wage. The time that politicians spend on minimum wage laws is time that is completely wasted; it's time that they could invest in doing things that really benefit their constituents.

The bottom line: any minimum wage laws passed should be local in nature and be automatically adjusted annually to inflation.

INTERNATIONAL GARBAGE

Canada and the US have an agreement on the transboundary movement of hazardous waste.

As a result, each year, approximately 992,000 tons of hazardous waste cross the Canada-US border on their way to recycling, treatment, or disposal sites in the United States.

Worldwide, the biggest producer of waste per capita is Canada, at 39.8 tons per year, 11 tons more per capita than the US.

I wonder if one reason for the elimination of Runway 18-36 at Willow Run Airport in Ypsilanti, MI is that, to land on Runway 18, a pilot would have to fly over a garbage dump constantly growing higher with garbage being dumped from Canada. Just wondering. Michigan has abundant landfills and low fees, making it a preferred destination for trash from other states and Canada. Michigan gets a lot of Canada's dirty diapers, coffee grounds, and banana peels.

One problem as far as restricting trash imports is that trash is a commodity under US law, and thus is protected from restriction both in terms of interstate and international commerce under the US Constitution's Commerce Clause, which basically doesn't allow discrimination between trash that originates from within a state to trash that originates elsewhere.

Trash obviously has an environmental impact on the landfills. There is groundwater contamination and noise pollution, and the odor is not something you could sell if you bottled it.

Would the US Supreme Court consider eliminating Commerce Clause protection of hazardous waste on environmental and health concerns? It's time to find out. Let's protect the planet and foster responsibility in garbage creation and disposal by making the people who produce the waste dispose of the waste.

The bottom line: Congress should pass a law mandating that each county in the United States be responsible for its own garbage disposal and that each county cannot export its garbage nor import any garbage from outside the county.

ABOUT THE AUTHOR

Sam Galanis's educational background includes a master's in international relations, a law degree (a member of the Michigan Bar for over fifty years but never practiced law and is now emeritus), and was accepted to medical school but decided not to go. The author was a financial advisor for over fifty-three years and was a senior institutional consultant to public pension plans with the internationally recognized designation of CIMA (Certified Investment Management Analyst). Sam retired at the end of July 2022. Sam is a pilot with multiengine and instrument ratings who owns and flies a Piper Cheyenne XXL aircraft (twin-engine turboprop), frequently on Wings of Mercy missions. Sam's upbringing emphasized being honest and helping and caring for others. Sam was always interested in commonsense solutions to areas of our economy and politics that can make life better and our country better.

www.ingramcontent.com/pod-product-compliance
Lightning Source LLC
Chambersburg PA
CBHW030806180726
47991CB00024B/1106